Get Off The Bench

Get Off The Bench

Kickstart Your Idea Now

Kerryn Vaughan

DISCLAIMER:
The information and material contained within this publication has been written and published solely for basic generalised guidance and inspirational purposes and is not meant for individual or business advice. Should any reader choose to make use of the information contained herein, this is their decision and the author and publishers shall have neither liability nor responsibility to any person or entity with respect to any loss, damage or injury caused or alleged to be caused directly or indirectly by the information contained in the book. It is recommended that the reader obtain their own independent advice.

First Edition 2019

10 9 8 7 6 5 4 3 2 1

Copyright © 2019 Kerryn Vaughan

All rights reserved. No part of this book may be reproduced or transmitted in any form or by any means whatsoever without written permission from the author, except for brief quotations used for reviews.

Cover illustration: Maira Giacoboni - Malugi-Art

Cover design: Kerryn Vaughan

National Library of Australia Cataloguing-in-Publication entry:

A catalogue record for this book is available from the National Library of Australia

Vaughan, Kerryn, 1963 -
    Get Off The Bench!: Kickstart your idea now / Kerryn Vaughan

    ISBN   978-0-9924275-1-1 (paperback).

        1.Self-development. 2.Goal setting. 3.Projects. 4.Personal achievement. 5.Team building.   I Title

Printed in Australia

Contents

Introduction
1. What's your big idea? (1)
2. Why oh why? (9)
3. What's in the way? (17)
4. Before you tell the world (27)
5. What's the problem? (33)
6. It's a pleasure! (39)
7. Risks (41)
8. Resources (47)
9. Show me the money! (51)
10. Connections & Collaborators (65)
11. Finding your tribe (71)
12. Resistance (85)
13. The right people are critical (89)
14. Brand, branding & logo (93)
15. Registering your project (101)
16. Chunk it, plan it, do it! (105)
17. Maintaining momentum (117)
18. And finally (121)
About the author (125)

Introduction

Got an idea or project you want to get off the ground? Or maybe you have many things running around inside your head, and you don't know where to start. This book is designed to help you breathe life into your idea and find the right people to support you.

So often we have a brilliant idea, but are plagued with feelings of self-doubt, or we just don't know where to start. Don't worry - most projects start precisely like that, and sadly some never get to see the light of day.

When I wrote my first book 'Magnificent Kids! - 23 Superheroes who are changing the world', I had absolutely no idea how to do any of it. I didn't know the first thing about publishing and certainly not about book formatting. I could have quickly abandoned the idea because I didn't have the answers or the knowledge, but I just started, trusting that each step would unfold - and it did!

I also remember creating One Planet Classrooms (OPC) which is now a Not for Profit (NFP), but didn't start out that way. It began as a Skype program between African and Australian classrooms.

I registered it as a business because I had no idea about how to register an NFP and assumed the process would be way over my head. I honestly didn't think I had the capacity to fully comprehend what it would take to set one up. But as I found out, that one wasn't so hard either. OK, hard but not impossible!

After several failures, OPC took on a whole new life. While I was interacting with teachers from schools in Africa, I discovered how many students were becoming very ill, some even dying, from drinking dirty stagnant water. It turns out that the failures were actually great opportunities in disguise, and so began a revised version of OPC.

We now support developing countries, predominantly Uganda, by supplying clean water solutions to schools and villages, facilitating heaps of projects like solar systems, mattresses, blankets, mosquito nets, clothing and food, as well as providing feminine hygiene solutions. We also initiate and support women's empowerment projects and, at the time of writing this, have over 180 kids in school as part of our student sponsorship program.

I asked a few trusted people to help me, and before long we registered as an NFP and haven't looked back. But imagine if I never started, or if I gave up after the Skype failure. Thousands of people would never have had the opportunities they have today, and my decision would have been responsible for that! Every project is worth the effort!

When you are clear on what it is you want to do, why you want to do it, and have the basics down, you at least have an idea of where you are heading.

Once you have a good overview, you need to take some action. Any action! A beneficial thing to remember is that action creates clarity. If things need to be revised down the track, that's OK, just get started. However, beware the trap of trying to have everything so perfect that nothing ever becomes of it.

The questions at the end of each chapter are designed to help you integrate what you just read, as well as help you gain more clarity, and then take another step. It would be best to read the entire book before reaching out to others, as there are some great pointers to help you reach out in a way that will win supporters, rather than turn them off.

I have used the words 'idea' and 'project' somewhat interchangeably, but ultimately, they mean the same thing. I've tried to use the word that provides a better context specific to the situation or topic. Throughout the book I have said it like it is without all the back-rubbing hoo-hah, so don't take it personally - just get on with it. In this game there's simply no room to be precious!

You might also notice throughout the book that I DON'T like fluffy words and I DO like exclamation marks!!!!! If you ever hear me speak in person, that will make perfect sense to you…

This book is designed to be a kickstarter for getting any idea off the bench and into the game, be it a personal goal, community project, business or social enterprise, or even the starting point for a larger Not for Profit with global reaches. If you want to make a difference with even a tiny-scale project, there are many things you can do that could have a significant impact on the lives you directly and indirectly touch.

However, it was never designed to cover everything in minute detail as that would be impossible. It depends how big and how complex you want to get as to which parts of this book might prompt you to delve further into specific areas. There's also no way to cover every type of project and every country, and while this book may help get business ideas off the ground, it should not be used as a comprehensive small business guide.

It was written primarily with community projects in mind, and all the chapters are relevant for this type of project. If you are going to involve other people, for example, volunteers, clients, beneficiaries and customers to name a few, or if there is going to be a financial exchange or turn over, then you really need to give consideration to every chapter. Of course, you can relax considerably if you just want to run a small book readers' group, for example, and require everybody to bring $2 to pay for milk, coffee and cake. You should just get it started and enjoy!

However, for other ideas or projects, it may well be that only some of the chapters are relevant. Projects like podcasting, blogs, vlogs, writing a book, a few friends knitting beanies and let's say a cat brushing group, probably don't need a lot of the serious stuff.

But that doesn't mean the idea or project is any less important. Whatever your idea, big or small, this book is a great starting point and should serve as a reminder that your project is important, and people need what you have to offer!

Get Off The Bench literally means get off the bench, get in the game, and don't sit around waiting for your turn. So now, let's get that idea out of your head, on to paper and get the first step underway.

Let's go!

"You will either step forward into growth or you will step back into safety."
~ Abraham Maslow

1

What's your big idea?

So, you have an idea that keeps running around in your mind. Some days it haunts you and shouts "Let me out of here!". Yep, I know the one! The one you think about every single day and just can't shake. If your idea is like that and pulling at your shirttails every day, then you have no choice - you must do it! Your inner voice is screaming that this is what you are meant to do.

On the other hand, if you have multiple ideas firing at you constantly, one of these things may be true for you:
- There is a brilliant idea amongst all the noise
- All the small ideas are actually pointing to one big idea (there is a common theme)
- You can possibly still do all of them, but it's best to focus on one at a time to actually achieve any (trust me!).

Spend a little time thinking about whether there is a theme running through the many ideas, and this might help to fine tune a bigger idea.

Regardless, the process is the same. If you can, grind it down to one idea just for the sake of working through this book. You can always go back and repeat the same process with any other ideas.

Remember this - the giant oak was once a tiny seed that somebody took the time to plant, nurture and believe in! Oh, and it was also a little nut that stood its ground! Something to keep in mind…

OK so let's work through a few questions and try to get some real clarity about the overview of your idea.

Your idea…

Try to be as specific as you can here, even if you are not entirely sure yet. Use your intuition and go with the first thing you think of (that's your gut talking) before your head kicks in and tells you 'you can't'. Don't worry if you don't have an exact picture yet; the fine-tuning will happen later.

Another way to get some clarity and filter through the noise and possible anxiety is to sit quietly with an idea and only focus on that. Notice how your body feels. If it feels excited and you feel strong and unstoppable, that's a good sign. You'll know if it feels right or not.

If it doesn't feel great in your body, then don't go with it, and do not pursue an idea if it's for the wrong reason. A great example of that is trying to prove something to somebody. Just don't do that; it uses way too much energy and takes you right off your own path.

If you can't narrow it down to just one idea, then maybe note down 3-4 that keep coming up in your mind. Hopefully, some of the remaining questions in the book will help you gain clarity.

Q. What idea would you like to get off the ground?

Your vision…

Hopefully, you started to see your idea unfold as you were doing the previous exercise. Now we want to look at the big picture. Let your imagination run wild. Imagine that nothing can hold you back, that everybody supports you and that you are actually doing your thing at its full potential. How does it look? What's happening?

Your vision may be something like:
- To provide education to every girl in Nepal
- To give backpacks filled with necessary items to every homeless child in your district
- To provide a clean water solution to every school in Rwanda

Q. What is your vision?

So much is possible…

How much we believe something is possible, determines how much effort we will put into it. Again, imagine yourself doing it. Can you see yourself doing it? The first question below asks **if** you think it is possible, and the second asks **how much** you believe it's possible. For the second question, mark where you are on the scale right now. It doesn't matter where you are currently, but if you want the idea to be successful, you need to put some energy into increasing your belief in the possibility. Right now, we are only considering **possibility**.

Here are a few ideas to help increase your belief:
- Visualise your idea's success
- Seek out other people who have succeeded in something similar
- Look at the traits, characteristics, skills etc. you have in common with others who are doing well with a similar idea
- Build on any specific skills or knowledge you feel you are lacking
- Dig deep and question any limiting thoughts or beliefs
- Remember that practice always trumps talent, so put the time in every single day

Even if it hasn't been done before, if you can see that it's possible, then it can be done.

The difference between where your idea is now and where you want it to be, is how much you believe it's possible!

I have a strong belief that if we can imagine it, it's already in our future waiting for us to collect. There's no point waiting for life to 'happen' to us when we have within us the power to create the life we want.

OK here goes…

Q. Is it possible? (yes or no)

Q. How much do you believe it's possible?

| 1 | 2 | 3 | 4 | 5 | 6 | 7 | 8 | 9 | 10 |

Q. What are you going to do to build on how much you believe it's possible?

You are the captain…

This next question is about your personal capacity to bring your idea to life. This could include physical capacity, intellectual capacity, mental stamina, resilience, knowledge, skills or anything else required to ensure the success of your idea. Can you build on your knowledge or skills? Or, can somebody else do some of the tasks while you remain in the driver's seat organising things?

Some people give up because they don't know everything that's required, but that's like throwing the baby out with the bath water. Please don't give up on your idea simply because you feel you can't do absolutely everything. You just have to be the captain!

Q. Can YOU do it? (Is it achievable?)

Chew on this - 97% of people give up too soon and work for the 3% who didn't!

IN A NUTSHELL…

What's your big idea?
- Your idea is valuable!
- Really imagine doing your thing
- You have to believe it's possible
- Be the 3%

"Never limit your vision based on your current resources."
~ Michael Hyatt

2

Why oh why?

Why?

You need to be clear about WHY you want to do this; in fact, the 'why' is much deeper than just this project. Your WHY is about your very being, the reason you exist. It should be about your values right at your core. It's not so much about the project WHY; it's about your personal WHY. If you said the 'why' is because 'people need it', that's not enough to satisfy potential supporters, nor is it enough to satisfy you to ensure the project has longevity and is deep and rich.

Your WHY has to be about something you believe in and have a basis in things like:

- Equality
- World peace
- Human rights
- Animal rights

- Education
- Anti-discrimination
- Conservation
- Quality service

It's to do with something at your core that's always stirred up whenever you are emotionally charged by something specific, good or bad. It's something you feel passionate about, and it doesn't have to be about saving the world. A point on that - nobody can save the world alone, so we should stop beating ourselves up about not doing 'everything'. We're not meant to do everything. It doesn't work like that; we just need to do something.

We are meant to do OUR thing, and our thing fits nicely into the jigsaw of life. Unfortunately, it's often the case that people want to do great things but become overwhelmed and disillusioned by not being able to resolve an issue entirely. It's like tipping out a 5,000 piece jigsaw puzzle and trying to put in all the pieces at once. You can't! But as each piece slowly goes in, you can see where the next piece fits and so on, and slowly we make progress until another jigsaw is complete.

A great example of that is slavery. No single person could have changed that alone, but several people decided to really own their pieces and bring them to the big puzzle. Eventually, that big one was complete. Imagine a separate set of puzzles for every issue in the world. Each small puzzle from each part of the world has to be put together first, then brought to the big puzzle, to have a global impact.

But even when that particular puzzle is complete, there are still thousands of issues remaining. Imagine trying to complete millions of complex jigsaws all at one time and expecting to succeed. You wouldn't and couldn't. That's why it's so critical we take responsibility for our piece and try to find those who have the other parts of the same puzzle. That's how progress is made.

So back to your 'why'. Here are some examples:
- Because animals are sentient beings who should be treated with compassion
- Because all children deserve to feel safe
- Because everybody should be treated equally
- Because people with disabilities should be seen for their abilities
- Because climate change is killing our beautiful planet and there is no planet B
- Because the colour of people's skin should be celebrated and diversity embraced
- Because the aged should be valued and have easy access to the community
- Because all customers deserve great service

A lot of these reasons exist simply because they are currently not being resolved or embraced. However, that being said, once you know what the issue or problem is, you must keep your focus on the solution. Staying focused on the problem brings actual physical discomfort, and that causes dis-ease within our bodies. That's not who we are meant to be.

We are meant to thrive and chase what we want, and frankly, most of us want peace, love and compassion. So, focus on that and align with that. Stay tuned into that and notice how different that feels physically, mentally, emotionally and spiritually.

Begin with asking yourself "Why do I want to do this project?", and go down as many WHY (or 'WHY is this important') layers as you need to, until you get to the core of you:

By the way, your WHY doesn't always have to be about other people or saving the world. It may well be that you're exhausted and have had an absolute gut full of the 9-5 grind. It might be something you have personally wanted to achieve for some time, but to date, have found every reason under the sun why you haven't achieved it yet.

So, if your project is a personal goal or a business idea, your WHY might look more like this:

Because I want:
- Flexible work hours
- Work / life balance
- Personal achievement
- More time with the kids
- Financial freedom

It's not selfish to want these things; in fact, more people should put these values first! The greater our own wellbeing, the more we can help others.

There are hundreds of reasons why we don't do things, but we really only need one reason why we should.

Q. What's your big WHY behind this project?
Note: it may be helpful to read the next part on purpose first, and then come back to this.

Everything is on purpose...

A lot of people get all caught up in trying to figure out what their purpose is. This is actually a very misleading exercise and one in which most people don't succeed. We spend a whole lot of time looking at 'things' we think could be our purpose, but these are just activities and not our purpose.

For example, people say things like "my purpose is to be a ...."

- Teacher
- Painter
- Photographer
- Life coach
- Writer
- Nurse

What if we view these things differently and see them as a type of vehicle that we're using at the moment purely to work within our purpose? Then what if we look at our 'why' (this can be bigger than just your project 'why') as our purpose?

This is a little deviation from your project, but let's say you feel drawn to several things - speaker, singer and podcast host. You start to tear yourself into pieces trying to decide which one you should follow as your purpose.

Eventually, years have passed, and you perceive you have not done any of them well, as you have continually dabbled in each, but not mastered any. Even worse, you feel you have completely missed your calling because you couldn't decide what you are 'supposed to do'. This is a very common story!

But if we reframe the story we are telling ourselves and living by, and reframe our perception of purpose, we can actually see we have been successful all along, and that we are already fulfilling our 'purpose'.

Go back to the 'why' for a minute. Now let's look at the three things - speaker, singer and podcast host. If you were to write each one as a heading across the top of a page with your 'why' underneath each one, you would likely find that the 'why' is the same across all three.

You may need to keep asking 'why' or 'why is this important' for several rows down until you get to a common 'why'. Just like doing fractions to find a common denominator.

For these three things, the bottom line might be something like 'to use my voice to spread messages of hope and to inspire people to take action'. When you find that common 'why', that's your purpose.

Then all you need to do is find activities to act as a vehicle for the purpose. No more beating yourself up and lots more joy spread into the world.

Q. What do you think your purpose could be?

IN A NUTSHELL...

Why oh Why?
- What's your big WHY?
- WHY has a number of levels
- We are meant to do our thing
- What's your purpose?

3

What's in the way?

So, what stops us from Getting Off The Bench? You would think if the idea is good enough and the world needs it, then there shouldn't be a problem. But there is! There is always some silly limiting belief or self-sabotaging behaviour that sticks to us like glue and no matter how hard we try we can't shake it. Even when we KNOW these things aren't true, or that they are ridiculous, they still hold us back.

Let's look at some of these things:

- Procrastination
- Sensing a lack of purpose
- Falling victim to the opinions of others
- Trouble committing to things
- Information overload
- Family and friends are not supportive
- Fear of criticism
- Comparing self to others

- Lack of motivation
- Unsure of where to start
- Negative self-talk
- Analysis paralysis
- Poor time management
- Lack of self-confidence
- Not willing to put in the hard work
- Unaware of personal power
- Lack of financial support
- Easier to follow the norm
- Not prepared to take risks
- Overwhelmed by the big picture
- Not able to break big tasks down into smaller chunks
- Fear of failure
- "Who am I to do this?"
- Succumbing to the expectations of others
- Not believing we're smart enough
- Fear of being caught out for not knowing what we're doing
- Can't see HOW things will unfold to succeed
- Fear of rejection
- Can't be bothered
- Perfectionism
- Not having anybody to be accountable to
- Self-doubt
- Feeling too young or too old

- Focused on past failures
- Fear of the unknown
- Imposter Syndrome
- Lack of clarity
- Not having access to the right resources
- Can't identify the first step
- Waiting to acquire ALL the information

Pretty impressive list hey? But it's not even an extensive list; there are tonnes of other reasons. It's just the tip of the iceberg. Underneath all of these is a whole world of beliefs, emotions and experiences that show up on the surface as behaviours, limitations and habits, that keep us from doing what we really want to do. Some of these things are real, and some are perceived, but either way, you will be surprised what you can achieve if you have the determination and courage to push past them. Even if you have doubt or are terrified.

"Courage is not the absence of fear, but rather the judgement that something else is more important than fear."
~ Ambrose Redmoon

There are loads of behavioural change strategies you could apply to any one of these things, but unless you take action, they are all useless.

So, the only sure-fire way to Get Off The Bench is to get started - one foot in front of the other, and just keep going.

If your WHY is big enough, the HOW will take care of itself. It's like having a non-motorised tram car and your WHY is 'because I need to get from point A to point B'. You won't get to point B just by sitting there looking at the tram car and wishing it to move. You have to push it!

At first, it's really difficult, and you just can't see how you are going to get it moving. But even an inch will help toward the momentum and one inch after another, before too long that tram car will start pushing itself along.

Soon it will gather so much momentum that you'll be running along behind with your arms outstretched trying to reach the back rails to pull yourself onboard. But you have to push through the pain to get it started.

The funny thing is that often the pain really isn't the pain you might imagine. In the above analogy, you can probably picture yourself busting a pooper valve trying to get that darn thing moving. All red in the face and almost passing out. But it's rarely a physical pain starting a project; it's the mental and emotional pain.

All the self-doubt and fear of 'what will people think?', and 'what if I fail?'. That's the pain you have to push through, and it's actually way more daunting than pushing through physical pain. Sorry!

But suppose for a moment you DO grit your teeth and squeeze your eyes shut and go for it. What if it's like one of those fake brick walls from a movie set? You get all prepared and build yourself up, then you grit your teeth and squeeze your eyes shut, and PUSH!

Then BAM!! All of a sudden you're through, and probably still trying to balance yourself because it was much easier than you expected. You dust yourself off and think "oh I wish I'd realised five years ago how simple that would be".

Guess what else you discover on the other side of that wall? People aren't criticising you, you didn't die from embarrassment, and people are actually cheering you on. You also found out that you CAN do it!

So, there's no time like the present to just get in there and back yourself. Clarity follows action and action cures fear. Just do the very first step, and the rest will sort itself out.

For the record, every successful person started somewhere. They weren't born perfect or with all the answers. They all took a chance knowing they could fail, and very often they did.

That's the way life works. It's not perfect, and neither are you, and nobody expects you to be. The person who tries is far more admirable than the one who never did; ultimately true failure is doing nothing.

But the truth is, you can NEVER have all the answers and have everything right before starting. It's impossible. If it were possible, you might as well just start at the most significant future point of your project. But you can't because you don't know what that is because it hasn't happened yet!

Imagine if Henry Ford never made the A model because he was waiting for it to be perfect. Waiting for the Mustang or waiting for the 2019 Fusion. He didn't say "no, I want it to have airbags and a blue tooth sound system and voice-activated ignition". He started with what he had and what he knew and built on that. Whether you like Fords or not, they have had a place on our roads since 1908. We made room for them, and there is also room for you!

Once you accept that you don't have to be perfect and never will be, you can relax and enjoy the ride - warts and all!

What's in the way?

Back to the tram car. Once you get that damn thing moving, the only way to keep it moving (after the initial dash to grab the back rail), is to take consistent, daily action.

If we went for a mad dash around the running track every couple of months but did no other running, we would run ourselves into the ground, and the exercise would be to no avail other than to make room for another donut! But if we go for a gentle run daily, we do a much better job at staying on track to feel better and reach healthier goals.

It's no different with a project. Daily habits win every time and daily practice always trumps talent. So, if you are feeling inadequate or that your possible lack of ability, skills or knowledge is putting you behind the eight ball, get doing things every day, and you'll end up the turtle and not the hare!

Daily practice also often trumps goal setting, as does accountability. There's a lot of evidence to suggest that if we have an accountability partner, we are 95% more likely to accomplish a goal compared to 40% probability if we only set a date to achieve it.

So, while we may have good intentions to achieve a goal, we are far more likely to succeed if we set up accountability appointments. **Who will you make your accountability buddy?**

But I just can't decide…

Another huge barrier to getting started is procrastination over which choice to make because you have multiple ideas and don't know which one is going to be successful. Forget it! You will never know that. How could you know that? There are no guarantees of success, but you are guaranteed to fail if you never try.

If you do have multiple projects you want to get started and can't make a decision, then you have 3 choices:

- Just choose one and get started - have a go and see where it leads you

- Start all of them but take a baby step each day and see which one starts to grow legs

- Do nothing at all! I bet this option makes you uncomfortable! Therefore, the only choices left are the other two. Now choose!

Whichever way you go, pay attention to your intuition, and look for evidence of success no matter how small.

Spoiler alert - If you start multiple projects, it's likely you won't be able to maintain momentum with all of them, so you need to be prepared to let some go. I recommend starting with one and doing one at a time. Start with the one that makes you the happiest.

Most people don't even start, if they think there is some chance they may have to let go. They fear looking like a failure, or that others will judge them for quitting. Nobody likes to be called a quitter, but we need to get over that. In reality, nobody is watching you that closely, and besides, you become yesterday's news very quickly.

If you screw up or quit, people might mention you over a coffee and say "Gee, Mary's thing didn't last long!". Then they will make assumptions for a couple of minutes and then move on to what their boss said or what the neighbour is doing or what they are having for dinner. Don't worry about those people! They are the same people who are sitting on the sidelines doing nothing except criticising others who are giving things a go. The world does not get better because of people like them. It gets better because of people like you who step up to the plate, even when you are scared, because you know the world needs what you have to offer.

Even if you don't know how it will work, or doubt that people will want it, or pay you for it, if it is in your heart and you can't shake it, then you need to try.

If you don't have a clear picture of where you're headed, you can always adjust your sails as you go. Let go of the fear and be messy – who cares? Just start and see where it goes. That's exactly what I did with this book, and it's still messy and far from perfect!

Today you get to choose - will you do the same thing you did yesterday and let the same things stop you, or will you step into your project?

> *"The way to get started is quit talking and start doing."*
> ~ Walt Disney

IN A NUTSHELL...

What's in the way?
- Have the determination and courage to push through
- If your WHY is big enough, the HOW will take care of itself
- Grit your teeth, squeeze your eyes shut and PUSH!
- Every successful person started somewhere
- You'll never be perfect so quit trying to be
- Daily practice wins every time
- Find an accountability buddy
- Today, choose to do things differently
- Just get started!

4

Before you tell the world

From here on in I will mostly refer to your idea as your project because if you answered the questions in the previous chapters, and you're still feeling excited, congratulations - you are now beginning your project!

Here are a few things you need to consider and perhaps trial, before telling the whole world:

- Begin at a grassroots level. Projects aimed at local, state, national or global issues can remain a grassroots project, which has more appeal to most people. They connect with the sense of local, community, ownership, belonging, and also offer an authentic and measurable way for people to see tangible outcomes.

- Consider your budget before asking for money. It's tough to get this right at the beginning, especially if you're thinking big picture, so start small. Try to estimate a rough budget for the first bite-sized chunk. It will be a lot easier to raise small amounts of money in the beginning, which will enable you to get some small successes under your belt. That's the evidence more prominent funders will be looking for if you intend to grow, so get a couple of runs on the board before you tackle the big guns.

- Find a variety of ways to tell your story, so it suits different audiences. This may mean using alternative language styles or designing specific presentations appropriate to the demographic. You need to be able to present equally as well to high-end business people as to your friends and family. Make sure it is relevant to them and pitch at their level. More on building a story later...

- Start small and choose something reasonably specific or niche that people can imagine or measure. Even if you have a big vision, pick a smaller chunk of it and trial it with just a handful of friends. When you are ready to enlist supporters, it will be much easier to get them on board if there is already something underway. It doesn't have to be big and elaborate; it just has to show that the project has the potential to grow legs and has already started crawling.

- If the project has such a big vision that you can't find a way to break it down into smaller chunks (particularly if it is still a concept), then you will have to sell YOU. People will need to be moved by YOU more so than the project as you are asking them to believe in YOU. That's a huge task if you don't already have some standing in your community or other relevant spaces. But that doesn't mean it's impossible. You will just have to find a way to build some fast credibility. Tip - genuine enthusiasm elicits curiosity.

- Get feedback - in casual conversation with people you trust, tell them your idea - "I've been thinking about this, what do you think?". You should welcome questions, opposing views and some resistance or pushback. This helps iron out any bugs that you may not have thought of and helps you see things from another perspective. It also gives you the opportunity to gauge what others might say (yes even in opposition) which allows you to fine-tune your responses. Always consider the possibility of integrating their feedback.

On the topic of feedback, if your idea or project is purely a personal goal, don't go telling the naysayers and criticisers. You already know what you want to do and you need to back yourself.

People need to understand the problem your project is aiming to address, as well as your proposed solution. They also need to feel they have the time or capacity to be able to be part of the solution and that it aligns with their values. This may be hard to sell if the vision is so big that it's potentially beyond the imagination or perceived capacity of the people you are trying to enlist support from.

I think every project has room to be broken down into chunks, so I highly recommend you give this the thought and effort it deserves. Particularly if you doubt you can sell YOU as the brand.

I talk quite a bit in this book about 'selling', and I make no apologies for it. Some people feel uncomfortable with 'selling' their project to get support, but how else could it work? If you don't sell, it will never grow, and you will be the one doing everything and paying for everything. Your project won't be sustainable.

More so, you have to stay focused on the very reason you started the project in the first place, what your values are and what your WHY is. What about the beneficiaries? Are you fighting for them or not, or is your project just a whim? I don't think it is, otherwise you would not be reading this book trying to figure out how to get things moving.

The other thing is that support doesn't just land in your lap. So, get comfortable with selling. Nobody gets upset with you for doing that unless you are rude and pushy, or if you are inappropriate and cheesy.

Just don't do those things; be genuine and show a real concern for the people you are trying to help - one foot in front of the other until you become good at it.

IN A NUTSHELL...

Before you tell the world
- Start small and choose a specific idea
- Make sure your vision is clear
- Consider keeping it at grassroots level
- Work out a rough budget before asking for funds
- Get feedback
- Make sure your story is suitable for different audiences

"Dream big.
Start small.
Act now."
~ Robin Sharma

5

What's the problem?

The problem is…

People will want to know your project is solving a problem. In fact, when it's time to recruit supporters they are more likely to come on board if they can clearly see a problem is being addressed, particularly one they have some emotional attachment to.

Social projects will be about humanity, animals or the environment (things that affect society en masse), and these projects tend to attract people with altruistic ideals.

These social issues appear to have an indirect effect on individuals, but those who support these types of projects have a deep understanding and awareness of how the problem, through a chain of events, eventually impacts each of us on a personal level.

There are also projects that address very local or niche concerns, and are likely to attract only people emotionally attached to that niche.

An example of this might be there is only one boat ramp at the local jetty and boat owners are becoming increasingly frustrated that it's taking over two hours to get their boat in the water. If your project addresses this problem, you will only attract people who are directly affected by that specific issue and have the hope that your project will solve their problem.

So ultimately both types of projects are valuable and affect individuals personally, and both have their place. You just need to be clear about the problem you are trying to solve, what your tribe might look like, and where you might find them.

Q. What problem are you trying to solve?

What's the problem?

Q. If this issue isn't solved, what are the implications or impact?

Q. How will your idea solve the problem and on what scale?

The benefits…

People want to see the benefits, and it's your job to sell them. To be clear, these benefits are for the beneficiaries of the project, not the interests of the supporters. We'll cover supporters in chapter 11 (Finding your Tribe). At first glance, you will see one significant overall benefit, but once you start to peel back the layers, you will probably notice there are a vast number of benefits. The benefits are also likely to extend well beyond the initial and direct beneficiaries so try to think bigger picture about your project.

A great example is connecting clean water to villages in Africa. The big picture benefit might be that people will stop dying from drinking contaminated water and that's fantastic. Another layer is that girls who would usually go to fetch water from stagnant ponds miles away, will not be subjected to sexual abuse en route and that alone opens up a whole plethora of other benefits.

Q. Who will your project benefit?

Q. What benefits can you foresee short term and long term?

> **IN A NUTSHELL...**
>
> **Problem solving**
> - Be clear about the problem and solution
> - Be clear about the benefits and sell them

"Leaders think and talk about solutions.
Followers think and talk about problems"
~ Brian Tracy

6

It's a pleasure!

While the last chapter was dedicated to solving a problem, which is what most social projects are about, there are also projects that cater to peoples' desires and pleasures. These are about kickstarting a project purely because you love something, and you think others will too.

If it's a project or side hustle where you intend to sell products or services, it's great to keep in mind that humans are far more interested in buying things they **want**, than things they **need**. If you need evidence of this, think about how long we put off going to the dentist, getting the car serviced or buying new tyres.

We need a warm coat but will likely come home with 3 shirts we didn't need because they look lovely and the whole coat searching thing got a bit tiring - besides 'I can buy that next week or the week after'! We definitely need new underwear, but that book says, 'let's have a lazy Sunday on the couch'.

We are quicker to buy coffee and cake than healthy food because it makes us feel fantastic - well until the immediate gratification wears off and then we promise we won't ever do it again - yeah right! The bottom line is we love to buy pleasure. We love our desires to be met and very often we impulse buy with extraordinary gusto!

There will also be ideas that are more voluntary, like running dance sessions at the local aged care facility or free yoga for the disadvantaged. These ideas are very valuable, not necessarily solving an identifiable problem, and will bring a lot of pleasure to very grateful people.

So, if your idea is all about candles, cupcakes, romantic experiences, getaways, boat rides, and gorgeous things that satisfy peoples' desires or bring pleasure, then you should go for it! There doesn't always need to be a problem to solve. Sometimes we just need rainbows and sparkles. Thank you for being a happiness crusader.

IN A NUTSHELL...

It's a pleasure!
- People buy what they want more than what they need
- Pleasure projects are much appreciated
- Happiness crusaders are awesome!

7

Risks

The basics…

In today's world, everything is about litigation. It shouldn't be, but it is, and some people could do with just taking their greedy little hats off. Regardless, you want to avoid this as much as possible! Besides the legal aspect, it's just morally right to make sure nobody gets hurt, and this includes animals and the environment. Sometimes risks and hazards are very obvious, but there may well be smaller ones that if not addressed could become massive issues.

Yes, I know - this is the killjoy chapter! Everybody is floating around on cloud nine, excited about their project, until they get to this bit. This area often sees people abandon brilliant projects unnecessarily, which is a crying shame. Most risks can be dealt with, but yes, we do have to put the serious hat on for this one. I'm tempted to say 'sorry!' but actually I'm not.

I don't want anybody getting hurt, and neither do you. Courtrooms are extremely unfriendly!

In this chapter, I won't go into too much depth as it's not my area of expertise. It provides a good basic overview, but you should do a lot more research yourself and be very thorough. The types of hazards and risks you may need to deal with depend on the specifics of your project.

A good rule of thumb is to imagine the worst-case scenario then consider how you could deal with it. Of course, worst case is unlikely to happen, but it's better to be prepared than very sorry if it did happen.

The obvious risks and hazards for projects are things like fire, crowds, traffic, electrocution, burns, sharps, physical strain, explosions, falling from heights, drowning, slipping or tripping, food poisoning, violence etc., but there are less obvious risks that are equally as important. Things like stress, fatigue, burn out, and exposure to things like chemicals, loud noises and bright lights.

Even less obvious, are things like financial risks and bullying but they are just as important nonetheless. Make sure you have something in place to both mitigate and effectively deal with them should they arise.

Permits & PPE…

If your project involves food, any volunteers will need to have their Food Safety or Food Handling certificates, and they must be current. You don't want people to get sick because of something you didn't do, and I certainly would not want to eat something handled by a person who didn't wash their hands after going to the toilet or blowing their nose. I imagine I'm not alone!

There will also be permits and a plethora of forms you need to get sorted with your local council if you are having a public event, so make yourself familiar with these. Don't let this put you off if your project depends on it, but you will have to jump through a few hoops.

Also, consider if your project requires people to wear Personal Protective Equipment (PPE). This includes things like gloves, face masks, goggles, hard hats, safety vests, gumboots, steel capped boots, knee or elbow pads, ear muffs or ear plugs, and overalls.

If your project requires people to wear PPE any more specific or complex than the basic protective gear, then it's likely you will need professional advice as that could indicate much higher risk activities.

Hazard or Risk...

The words 'hazard' and 'risk' are often used interchangeably, but they are different things. Here's a brief overview of the words used in this area:

Harm - physical injury or damage to health (this can include death)
Hazard - a potential source of harm
Risk - the combination of the likelihood of the occurrence of harm and the severity of that harm
Likelihood - the chance of something happening

A risk assessment identifies hazards, analyses and evaluates the associated risks, and then determines the best way to eliminate the risks. Sometimes the risks can't be eliminated, so they need to be either controlled or reduced.

It would be wise to Google a risk assessment matrix, so you can determine the level of risk you might potentially be dealing with.

If after completing a risk assessment matrix, there are risks that rate any higher than 'low-risk', I would certainly seek legal advice, or at the very least, engage the services of a professional Occupational Health and Safety consultant.

Even with low-risk hazards, I would make sure these are well documented and that anybody who is even remotely likely to be affected, is made aware of the hazards and the potential to impact their life permanently, should something extreme happen. It would be a good idea to have some legal document drawn up to cover all parties.

Insurance...

I strongly suggest you research Public Liability and Professional Indemnity insurance in case you need either or both of them. In brief, Public Liability insurance protects you against claims of personal injury or property damage to a third party as a result of your business activities. Professional Indemnity insurance protects you from being sued for damages arising from your advice or services.

Please note these explanations are only brief overviews and are not meant to be taken as word for word legal definitions. You should investigate both of these to determine if they apply to your project, but it is likely you will need Public Liability insurance at the very minimum. Both are reasonably affordable.

Now that we've covered the basics, have a go at this template:

Get Off The Bench!

Q. What hazards & risks do you foresee and how can you mitigate them?

Hazard	Risk level (use a risk assessment matrix)	Action(s)

IN A NUTSHELL...

Risks
- Identify all hazards and risks
- Put things in place to eliminate or reduce them
- Consider insurance

8

Resources

You will probably need some resources to set up your project. These resources might be as simple as a laptop, printer and mobile phone, or they might be very complex and expensive. Either way, the right resources are a big part of any successful project.

To begin with, think about all the resources you may need and make a list of them. Include all the things you already have so you can make a comprehensive list of everything you need. This will help you tick things off as you acquire them and will also be useful when asking for donations or support.

Every project is going to be different and require resources specific to their individual needs, but to get you thinking here are a few examples:

- Finances
- Buildings and infrastructure
- Venues or office space

- Access to printing
- Sports equipment
- Website
- Data projector & screen
- Bus
- Safety equipment
- Gardening equipment
- Business cards
- Books
- Commercial kitchen

Q. What resources do you need?

Q. Which of these resources do you already have?

Q. Where can you get the outstanding resources?
(Friends, family, community, key supporters, sponsors, government, grants, crowdfunding, fundraising)

IN A NUTSHELL...

Resources
- Work out the resources you might need
- Consider what you already have
- Where could you get the balance?
- Think about your connections and what they might have access to
- You don't need brand new things to get started

9

Show me the money!

Budgeting…

If your project requires money to either come in or go out, you will need a way to manage that, but you will also need avenues to obtain money. The first thing to do is to create a draft budget. Even if you don't know for sure how much money you will need, you still have to start somewhere.

Your vision will give you some idea about what you imagine you will need to spend money on, at least for project spending. For example, if you wanted to feed the homeless, you would need to start by considering what you would like to feed them, how much each meal will cost, how many people you think you will need to feed, how you will deliver the meals, and if this delivery will cost the project or if it will be volunteers funding themselves to deliver.

This draft budget will serve as your foundation, but you can expect to review and refine it often.

Staying with this scenario for a moment, in an ideal world, you would feed every person in need a lovely roast every night that costs $12 from a local cafe, delivered by an unlimited number of volunteers who want to do this every night, and everybody is happy.

But that's probably not realistic or sustainable, and particularly when you are just starting. You have to be prepared to both build the project and also be a little creative when it comes to what's coming in and what's going out.

A more realistic starting point is that a small handful of your family or friends will help out by making sandwiches, or another cheap alternative in their own kitchens using food they have paid for themselves.

But this excitement is likely to fizzle out if help doesn't arrive soon. Most people love to jump in and help, but compassion fatigue is a real thing. So where to from here?

Initially, this is a great starting point. What it provides is an excellent opportunity to measure and assess how things are going and what is needed to make the project sustainable.

You gather feedback from the volunteers and also from the people you are providing food for. The feedback highlights the volunteers are burning out and becoming less willing to forego their personal cash, time and fuel.

So, you would need to address this. The people you are supporting with food are probably less likely to complain, but jam sandwiches might be getting a little hard to swallow after three months!

This has given you the opportunity to get some figures, and now you will need to review that draft budget. Once your numbers are more accurate and you have some evidence under your belt, you can start reaching beyond your handful of volunteers and try to obtain funds.

You will also need to consider if there needs to be fuel reimbursement and any other running costs. These are often overlooked and paid for by the project initiator, but this soon runs you thin. This took me a long time to learn myself!

So, let's look at where you can obtain funds from, other than friends and family.

Grants…

Most grant applications will not even consider you without a very clear vision of what you intend to spend the money on and how it will solve a problem. They will ask for detailed information, and it helps if you already have some pilot evaluations to submit as evidence.

They want to know how their money is going to be used and they want to see that you have a way of managing that money effectively.

There is so much money out there, and numerous funding bodies want to support projects. However, you need to make sure that the grant you are applying for is well matched to what you require, or you will have wasted a lot of time filling in the forms, and many are incredibly cumbersome.

The quickest way to begin your search for grants is to just Google 'grants Australia', or whatever your country is. A multitude of websites will come up, and then you're off and running.

Some of these websites may ask you to become a member for a fee as they act as a one-stop shop for hundreds, if not thousands of grants.

Then there are other platforms that offer smaller specific grants, and you can start submitting straight away. Often your local council will have grants for community projects, so don't overlook them.

Another great way to find grants is to ask people you know. It's surprising how many people know things you wouldn't even think of!

Most grants are very specific, and a lot are very localised. If it's not right for you, move on and find the one that is. Please read the information for each grant thoroughly.

When you start looking at grants, you are likely to be put off by the requirements, but keep in mind some people specialise in grant writing, so don't be afraid to utilise them, or at least have some conversation with them.

Sponsors...

Sponsors are businesses or organisations that give you some funding in exchange for their name being advertised or promoted in some way.

Generally, the more the sponsor provides, the more publicity they get in return, but it really is about making a deal you and the sponsor are both happy with.

Sometimes a project will promote a business or organisation as a sponsor because they provided something other than cash.

Examples of this might be printing promotional material for an event, transport or accommodation for guests, donated gifts for you to use as prizes at an event and so on.

Whatever the exchange, a sponsor will want their name in lights and rightly so as they are playing a significant role in helping you achieve your goal.

Partnerships…

Partnerships provide a wonderful opportunity to be creative and resourceful. In some cases, partnerships will be very similar to sponsorships, so it's about the deal you make together.

Partnerships are often in-kind - some way the partner can add value to your project but not necessarily with cold hard cash. It might be networking value, or they may offer their name to be used in conjunction with your project which will give it more credibility, or maybe offer to promote you through their email list.

The pay-off might be promoting their name as you would with a sponsor, but it could also be an exchange of service. For example, they promote you through all their channels if you build a website for them, or maybe run a workshop for their employees.

There are literally hundreds of ways to build great partnerships so don't be shy - the worst thing that can happen is they say no. With all partnerships, it's a two-way exchange - you must give something in return.

Fundraising…

Fundraising is often a vital part of the project. You can't rely on the government or philanthropic organisations to be in love with, or in line with your project.

Nor can you rely on sponsors or partners. Yes, you may get some great support, but most projects are self-funded through fundraising activities and events.

At One Planet Classrooms we hold an annual fundraiser where supporters buy a ticket to attend, and we include a few presentations on what we have been up to, so the attendees can see the evidence, but we also have raffles and auctions on the night. To obtain prizes, we ask local business and individuals if they would like to donate something. Most say yes, and then we promote them.

These donations include football jumpers, paintings, vouchers, jewellery, candles, wellbeing packs, books and many other things that add value to the attendees. We also have live music and a whole lot of fun.

If you are going to host an event, you will need to budget for the cost of the venue, food, music, photographer and any other relevant expenses. You can quite often get friends to organise or supply some of this cheaply, or free for a good cause. Again, there may be an exchange.

If you are selling tickets, there are loads of online ticket platforms, and most are reasonably easy to use, but in my experience, they all need a bit of playing around with to find everything. They do take a small fee, but the ease of online ticketing is well worth it.

Don't forget to include the ticket link on your social media, website and in your emails and any other form of electronic correspondence. If you are handing out printed fliers, it's easier for potential attendees if you just send them to your website to find the link. But make sure the link on the website is very easy to find.

There are also many ticket printing businesses if you want to sell hard tickets. Just do some exploring, and you'll be surprised at how much is available at a very reasonable price.

I'm not sure how other places work, but in Victoria, if you expect to raise more than $10,000 per year through fundraising, you will have to register as a fundraiser with Consumer Affairs Victoria. Please make sure you check out what is required in your neck of the woods because you could find yourself breaching rules you don't want to. This could be costly!

Fundraising opportunities are only limited by your imagination or your will to get out there and make it happen, but also keep in mind that there are literally hundreds of thousands of other projects vying to get funds into their accounts.

Donors are wanting to know what their money is paying for so be ready to have information at hand and also a website or something similar where they can see some evidence.

There are hundreds of fundraising ideas on the internet so get Googling!

Crowdfunding…

Crowdfunding is more for just one-off fundraising campaigns, and mostly crowdfunding is used to kickstart projects or ventures. Basically, it's lots of people giving small amounts so you can reach your target, and it's predominantly done via the internet.

You work out how much you will need and what the money will be spent on, and then you build a pitch to win supporters. At any one time, there are tens of thousands of crowdfunding projects trying to get your attention.

If you put a campaign on a crowdfunding platform and hope people will find it while they are browsing that website, it's very likely they won't. You need people who will share and promote your idea widely, and usually, this means people with your own community of followers.

A great crowdfunding success story is the Flow Hive. Cedar Anderson and his father Stuart are beekeepers from Australia who designed the Flow Hive as a faster and easier way to harvest honey. They put the campaign on Kickstarter and hoped to raise around $100,000 to buy the equipment needed to make the hives on a more economical scale.

Their idea was so well received they made $16.9 million in eight weeks and were completely overwhelmed by the response. The best part is the Flow Hive is gentle on the bees!

But don't get too excited - these success stories are few and far between and most only raise a few thousand and only if they do it right.

Mostly the crowdfunding money comes from fans and friends of the project or campaigner. Carol Tice, a guest writer for Forbes, says you have to have at least 4 of these 5 elements to be successful:

1. You have an audience
2. You offer something truly groundbreaking
3. You market the heck out of your campaign
4. You create a fascinating video (not cheap, and one people will want to share)
5. You have exciting rewards

So, there you have it. Yet another way to raise funds if you're game!

One final thing for this chapter - it's always best to find partners, sponsors, funders and donors who share the values of your project, or at the very least, don't conflict with them.

Q. Jot down some ideas about where you could potentially source funding or partnership support for your project…

IN A NUTSHELL…

Show me the money!
- Create a draft budget and have a good idea about how the money will be spent
- Read grant guidelines very carefully and make sure it is a good match for you
- Sponsorships and partnerships are a two-way exchange
- There are hundreds of ways to fundraise but make sure you stand out, and register if you are required to do so
- Successful crowdfunding requires a great deal of promotion from your family, friends and followers

> "There's no shortage of money in this world. Start hustling."
> ~ Grant Cardone

10

Connections & Collaborators…

Connections - these are people you can collaborate with to build the project, or people you recruit once the project is underway. Let's imagine your project as a sailing ship. You first need to get it built; this is where connections and collaborators come in. They help you build the ship, but they also step in here and there to help maintain it.

We all have connections who:

- Have skills and talents that would be very useful
- Are connected to other people who would be very useful
- Have a great 'can do' attitude regardless of skills and talent
- Are extremely resourceful

- Take a little more time to come on board, but once they believe in something they are unstoppable
- Who will back you no matter what
- Who are prepared to back you blindly but can turn out to be rogue wild cards (avoid these people if possible)

While it's impossible to cover every single type of person, the above will give you a good start, and you can always add more as you think of them. It's also impossible to know exactly how people will behave or contribute until they are actually on board, but if you have seen somebody in action previously, that's usually a good measure.

A great question to ask the really eager people is 'why do you want to get involved?'. You may need to read between the lines, but it's often a good start when trying to determine who is wanting to support you for the right reasons.

It's very important to know who's who and what they have to offer, however good karma and good business always require a genuine exchange of value to work effectively. So, think carefully about how you might be able to make mutually beneficial deals. Do not 'use' people or you will very quickly become unfavourable.

Whether you are requesting something from an established connection, or a stranger, be clear about what you are asking for. People are not mind readers, and in such a busy world nobody has time to waste trying to read between the lines, or to go back and forth with you to establish some clarity about your request. People will not search for missing information.

Keep in mind that people are really busy, so your request has to either benefit them or be something that can offer very little interference to their schedule.

If you're asking for money, be very clear about how much you want, when you want it, and the impact the supporter's money will make. While there are some very wealthy people out there who you might think 'they can afford it' or 'why wouldn't they want to help?', remember in most cases they worked very hard for their money, and they know how to spend it wisely. Nobody will throw their money at you; you'll have to work for it.

Use the power of story, give real stories as examples and clearly show how problems can be solved. People love to be the hero of the story but keep in mind that Superman never went to the phone box unless he was clear that somebody was in trouble!

Q. Who do you know? What could you ask them for?

Who do you know?	What could you ask them for?

Connections & Collaborators

Q. Who do they know?

IN A NUTSHELL...

Connections
- Think about who you know and what they can offer. Further, who are they connected to? This doesn't mean you can 'use' them and you have to respect their decision if they say no, particularly if you are asking for money.
- People love to be the hero of the story, but keep in mind that Superman never went to the phone box unless he was clear somebody was in trouble!

"All the knowledge is in the connections."
~ David Rumelhart

11

Finding your tribe

Your tribe are those who support you and keep your project alive. They are the volunteers and helpers, and often the ones who voluntarily take on the role of 'spreading the word'. Thinking back to the sailing ship analogy, these are the people who keep the wind in your sail. Your project relies on them, and they need to feel valuable.

People don't just jump on board because they like you. Yes, your reputation and their past experience of dealing with you will make a difference, and if you are trusted and reliable, you are on the way.

But even if people show some interest, they still need to:

Listen to your idea
Keep in mind their interpretation of it will be influenced by their own knowledge and experiences, so be very clear about what you are trying to convey.

Understand the concept

People want to know all the ins and outs, and that's fair. The project is YOUR baby, so you will have spent a long time thinking about it from every angle and some of the information and logistics you will likely take for granted.

So, make sure you get feedback and determine if there is anything else you need to clarify. Keep the information clear, but as brief and straightforward as possible as you will lose people if the information is too complicated. Oh, and don't use flashy words!

Feel a connection

People will not invest themselves in anything unless they are emotively moved or feel a sense of connection. This is where good storytelling can really enhance your project. Can you tell them a real-life story that will make them feel something, and is something they can personally relate to?

You may be wanting to start a project that supports girls in Africa who are married off at 12 years of age and who are subjected to a life of hell at the hands of older men, while constantly living with infections and lack of medical care. Most people in developed countries don't live this existence so they may struggle to connect.

But if you were to tell the story of just one girl, they may start to imagine how it would feel if she was their daughter, or they might relate it to a close friend who suffers from abuse, or perhaps to a documentary that touched them deeply. It is then they decide to help, and they are motivated by compassion and empathy, and by the realisation they have the capacity to change this girl's life in some way. Being genuine is more important than being intelligent. If it comes from your heart, it has a greater capacity to connect.

Take action

People only take action when they feel strongly about the person or the idea; however, they may not take action without all of the above being fulfilled. You might be lucky enough to win a couple of supporters even if they feel they only have a percentage of the information and believe they will learn more as they go; however, they will still need to feel there is something in it for them in order to be motivated.

People want clear direction so make sure you have this worked out prior to asking them to do something. They don't follow blindly, at least not for very long!

Whatever it is you are asking people to do, it needs to fit seamlessly into their lives and give them a sense of joy and satisfaction, and also appeal to their commitment to charitable deeds.

It should not cause any disruption or major inconvenience and cannot be perceived as a chore. Ultimately you are asking them to trade their precious time (time they can never have back), so it needs to be worth their while and they need to feel it is adding value to their own lives in some way.

Get good at storytelling

People love stories. We consume stories endlessly through television, radio, movies, dance, books, art, theatre, podcasts, music, social gatherings, and many types of cultural ceremonies and rituals. We can never get enough.

Stories are the quickest and easiest way for people to connect to the characters, stirring emotion and empathy. Essentially, they feel like they are a part of the story, and that has real connection value.

Very often it makes them feel great; maybe it's escapism, a call to action, or an opportunity to be the hero. Whatever it is, it works.

Turn your project into a story about who you are helping and why. If you are able, use images to assist with the storytelling as the brain processes images around 60 times faster than words, and images more effectively help us remember facts and feelings.

A good story should be a linear experience for the listener, including:

1. Who the main character is - *this would be the beneficiary (this could be a group)*
2. What they want or need
3. Why they don't have it
4. How they can get it
5. Outcome (the win)

Does your story include:
- Emotion?
- Something from a true story to make it come to life?
- A way to make the listener feel what you felt?
- Education and entertainment (this may include drama)?
- A way for the person to be the hero of the story?

Let's look at your story board:

Q. Who is the main character?

Q. What do they want or need?

Q. Why don't they have it?

Q. How can they get it?

Q. What do you anticipate the outcome to be?

Reaching out to your tribe

We are the most connected we have ever been regarding technology, which means there's an abundance of opportunities and mediums available for reaching out to people. While many criticise social media platforms, and a lot of the time they deserve just that, they do make it very easy to connect with others.

In the past, we were limited to things like ads in newspapers, letterbox drops, and posters in shop windows. At least these were the more affordable ones, but they still cost money that was often hard to come by. The next level up was radio and television and the cost of these made it impossible for most people.

Today we can reach thousands of people for free or at a very minimal cost through social media, websites, blogs, podcasts, vlogs and email, to name a few. You can even precisely and cheaply target your audience through social media. The cost of building a website is also inexpensive and easy to maintain yourself with only a small amount of guidance. You just have to put a bit of time into learning it, and you're off and running. But no matter how you do it, you need to have a solid online presence, and people must be able to find you easily. They will not be bothered trying to hunt you down.

Technology aside, there are still many other things that help you reach your tribe. These might be personal skills and strengths that help you connect with people. Perhaps an active network you are a part of, maybe you have a strong local profile, or you might have skills in communication, public speaking, writing, or graphic design for instance.

You might have a story that has excellent impact value. All of these things can help you reach your tribe. So, let's look at what you have:

Q. What strengths/skills/channels (including technology), do you have that could help connect your idea to your tribe?

Finding your tribe

It's a really good exercise to visualise your tribe. Who are they and what do they look like? Are they older, younger, or a variety of ages? Are they gender specific? Are they predominantly interested in animals, humanity or the planet? Are they from specific cultural communities? Are they local, state, national or global? The list goes on.

It's important to find people who resonate with your message. These are the people you won't have to waste precious time on, or work hard to convince.

Once you have fine-tuned who your tribe might be, think about where you can find them? Where do these people hang out? Are they likely to be already volunteering in the community, online warriors, part of a community group, members of a niche group, travellers, part of a women's network, business owners, teachers?

Start targeting your campaign in those areas first. It's also likely they will know others, who know others, who would like to be part of your project.

Of course, you won't find everybody in these niche places and nor will every supporter look the same or like the same things, but it's a great place to start.

Q. What does your tribe look like?

Q. Where do they hang out?

Return on investment

There are very few people who will invest without expecting something in return. Most say they don't want anything, but often they do. That something is usually not money unless we are talking about a financial backer, and then you'd better be very clear about how they are going to be repaid, or what exchange needs to be agreed upon. For everybody else, it's more about the vibe and being in alignment with their values.

Everybody is looking for something to make them feel good (especially about themselves), or for something that will help them with personal or professional development. This includes the buzz they get from helping somebody else.

Some returns might be connection, self-esteem, self-worth, reputation, networking, recognition, sense of belonging, appreciation, security, feeling seen, feeling valued, friendship, skill development, personal development, leads or recommendations for their own business, advertising or promotion. Achievement and success also provide a great deal of satisfaction and support and help to build a more positive personal story.

Desired rewards are more often things that serve our individual value system, rather than financial gain.

Q. What is the return for the investor?
(anybody who gives anything)

Investor/Investment	Return

Finding your right tribe is a slow and steady process and won't happen overnight, but in the long run, it will be well worth the effort. There is some great truth in 'your tribe will find you', but you have to have a solid online and physical presence to be visible to them. You also need to gain trust and confidence.

Q. Anything else you want to note about your potential tribe?

Finding your tribe *IN A NUTSHELL...*

To get people on board they need to:
- Listen to your idea
- Understand the information
- Feel a connection to the project or you
- Take action

Your story needs to have:
- A strong storyline around a character (or group) and provide a way for your tribe to be the heroes
- A strong emotional connection to the listener

The investor must have some return

12

Resistance

Be prepared for resistance!

If somebody has resistance, determine how vital their support is to you and the project. If you are expending a lot of energy chasing and trying to convince them, but the outcome is unlikely to amount to much, let them go and stop wasting your time.

On the other hand, if their support is essential then connect with them, try to understand who they really are, and find the source of the resistance. Don't try to manipulate that, but rather provide stable and reliable information and have a genuine conversation. Get to know who they are and what matters to them before bombarding them with your idea.

There are a whole lot of reasons why people resist ideas, and most of them revolve around fear. Fear of failure, fear of something new, fear of change, fear of their position or status being impacted, fear of their environment being altered, to name a few.

The other main reason is confusion - you need to be clear about what you are trying to achieve, the problem you want solved, and how to achieve that outcome. People back off or resist if they can't understand something.

We are all like that. If somebody says "get in the car" the first thing we say is "Why? Where are we going?" before we get in. Or when you plan a holiday, you don't just pack a bag and head to the airport without knowing your destination.

It's the same thing - people want clarity. You also have to keep in mind that in this day and age spare time is rarely abundant, so have the road map ready with all the landmarks clearly drawn.

You might also consider whether your project would be best run as a pilot program, so people don't feel they have to commit to a long-term project, particularly if there is some resistance. A pilot program gives you the opportunity to showcase your project and gain evidence of successful outcomes. People are then more likely to jump on board because of the success, and at the end of the day, people do want projects to succeed.

However, if the pilot program fails or falls short, you can go back to the drawing board and iron out all the things that didn't work. It doesn't matter if things didn't turn out as planned, because that provides the opportunity for review and to try it a different way.

Many roads lead to the same destination, so just choose another road or slightly alter your destination. Don't abandon your idea just because there were some shortfalls. Fix them and get back on the bike - this builds resilience, and you're going to need a whole lot of that!

Q. Is your idea the type that would be best run as a pilot in order to gain evidence and trust?

Q. What outcomes would you need to measure to provide evidence of success?

> **IN A NUTSHELL...**
>
> **Resistance**
> - You WILL get resistance
> - Fear and confusion cause the most resistance
> - Be very clear about what your project aims to do and how people can help
> - Consider a pilot program to build evidence and credibility

13

The right people are critical

When you have the right people on board, let them be part of the expansion and momentum of the project. When people are encouraged to contribute, and they feel they are being listened to, they will invest in the project more - physically, mentally, emotionally and spiritually. People like to feel a sense of ownership, and they love feeling trusted.

While there are some people who do need to be supervised, for a whole variety of reasons, most people like to work autonomously, and it's amazing what they come up with if given a chance.

It is common for project initiators to feel a sense of fear or dread around letting others have some influence, and the most dread comes from the concern that these people will become wayward and send the project off on a completely different tangent.

There is a massive tendency to hang on to that baby so damn tight because it's 'mine'. But try to imagine that picture as a real baby you are squeezing the life out of. Children become the adults they do because of how many people influenced their lives as they were growing. Think of your project in the same way. If you want it to develop and expand, it really might need a village to nurture it.

However, there is a small percentage of people who do love to jump in after the hard work is done, do a few small things and somehow convince people they were massive things, then direct all the credit to themselves. Fortunately, these people are few and far between, but they are an absolute nightmare within small projects and organisations. Further, once these people have a foot in, they tend to bring followers.

Your project can very quickly end up with a number of cliques, and ultimately that will do insurmountable damage to your project and reputation. These people are very hard to get rid of, so it's important to choose wisely in the first place and be quick to put a halt to rogue activity.

The best protection you can have is to be crystal clear about your vision, values, the exact problem you are solving, and any other specifics that help to keep people focused on the vision and desired outcomes. Also have clear written rules or guidelines.

A good rule to remember is that when people feel they have some ownership and can see progress, they will bring others. So, focus on the people who are going to deliver value to the project, and remember to say 'we' more than you say 'I'.

In the last question in this chapter, I talk about non-negotiables. These are the things you will not budge on. The things you are not prepared to have or not have within your project. It's kind of like making that list for the perfect partner!

Q. What values do you have in common with people you might want to support you?

Q. How can these values be connected to your project?

Q. What are your non-negotiables (things you absolutely won't budge on)?

IN A NUTSHELL...

The right people are critical
- Let supporters be a part of the expansion and momentum of the project
- People invest more if they feel heard, seen and appreciated
- Be very clear about your vision and desired outcome, so people stay on track
- People who feel connected and involved will bring others
- Say 'we' more than you say 'I'
- Be clear about your non-negotiables

14

Brand, Branding & Logo

I want to be clear that I'm not an expert on brands or branding and have never claimed to be. How I wish! This is quite a complex area to get your head around but very important for your project. A lot of people associate brands and branding with only 'for profit' businesses, but it's just as important for Not For Profit's, community groups and charities.

Brand

Your brand is about how your customers perceive you and often gives rise to an associated emotion. It's the promise you make to your customer, and it should reflect your values. It's about the relationship and EVERY interaction you have with your customers and partners and is more important than your products and services. It's about how you treat people and how consistent you are with your messages and performance; this goes right down to the people you have working for you. Or in the case of a project, your tribe.

Every member of your tribe needs to be aware of the project's values and about how you want to be perceived, because if they are not behaving in a way that the customer expects of the brand, you will lose the customer. They will not have faith in you. Your brand even goes right down to how you answer the phone! Basically, the image you project for your brand has to ring true.

When creating a brand think about what you excel at (your point of difference) and what you believe in (your values). Your customer will expect you to deliver these every time. But these things also need to match customer requirements, or they will only exist for your benefit. Every touch point for the customer should look and feel the same.

If you think about brands such as McDonald's, Coca Cola, Mercedes, to name a few, the thing that stands out is consistency. It doesn't matter where in the world you buy from one of these brands, you always get what you expect. Whether you like them or not, this reliability works. By the way, I have no affiliation with any of them!

If YOU are the brand, you need to walk your talk. You need to be clear about what you stand for and that your behaviour aligns with that.

Branding

Branding is about how you use your image to influence and manage the way people perceive and respond to your brand. It's about creating loyalty and an emotional connection with the customer. Branding is also about maintaining and strengthening your brand, and if needed, reviewing and changing it to better fit what customers are looking for.

That's a basic overview of branding, and rather than try to fill this space with fluffy words (which I don't like to do) I recommend heading over to this Canva link and taking a look at how emotional branding works.

https://www.canva.com/learn/emotional-branding/

Logo

Your logo is like the foundation of your brand. It's the visual graphic that people see that makes them instantly recognise and connect to you, and everything about your project should display your logo. If you have a trusted brand, your customers will feel a sense of reliability and security when they see your logo. It communicates your brand, so it's important to have one that reflects it well.

You can even create one yourself with a logo making program or other graphic design programs as the cheapest option. There are also freelancing platforms like Fiverr, 99 Designs, and Upwork where you select a designer and ask them to design something for you, or you submit your request, and graphic artists compete for your work.

These are well priced and a good option for a budget, but sometimes it can be hit and miss at the cheap rate. Another point to add is that while they might be great graphic designers they are not necessarily branding experts, so may miss the connection between the logo and the brand. However, I have seen many a good design come from these platforms, so I guess it's up to you to communicate clearly what you are looking for.

The illustration on the front cover of this very book was designed by Maira Giacoboni (Malugi-Art), a graphic artist from Argentina, contracted through Fiverr. I love her work! There would also be a lot of aspiring artists living in your own neighbourhood who might be able to help. The higher-end option is to pay a graphic designer or a branding expert, but this will cost a whole lot more, and when you are just starting your project, the budget might be too slim. You have to find the right fit for you.

You will need a high-resolution logo so if you use an online platform make sure you don't be a cheapskate and only pay for the low-resolution version or one with a watermark. People don't trust anything that looks substandard. There are a number of file types you can use, but for this, we will just look at two of the most commonly used, PNG and JPG. Proficient graphic designers might be horrified with me saying that, but I want to keep this simple and usable for everybody.

The easiest way to be compatible with most programs and partners is to have a high-resolution PNG file with a transparent background. This might not seem that important, but if you are partnering with somebody and they are going to display your logo on their coloured banner, a PNG logo will sit nicely over any colour. Well, as long as the colours match!

PNG files also have better image compression technology, so if compressed they don't lose quality.

If your logo is a JPG/JPEG file, it will commonly have a solid square or rectangular background, and on a coloured banner, your logo would be a box containing the logo rather than the logo itself being the main visual focus. A JPG file can also lose quality if compressed.

As I said, I am trying to keep this simple, and computer talk is not everybody's strength, so I recommend chatting with a computer whiz who will easily be able to show you the options.

The reason your logo needs to be high resolution is so that it always looks sharp and clear no matter where it is placed or how it is used, particularly if it is enlarged. There is nothing worse than seeing a fuzzy logo, and people will immediately assume your project is cheap and unprofessional. It's a very easy fix so get it right from the beginning.

When designing a logo, you need to consider how you might encompass the values of your brand, and it's always best to have a good understanding of your target market. For example, a community project logo will often have people in it to reflect inclusion as one of its key values, whereas some sporting logos reflect personal power and achievement.

Colours are also psychologically important, so it would be wise to do some research around logo colours.

It's worth putting a fair bit of thought into your logo as it can be business suicide to change it once you become established and have a great reputation, particularly if your current logo is well recognised. Investing time (and money) to get your logo right from the start is well worth it.

IN A NUTSHELL...

Brand, Branding & Logo
- Your brand is how your customers perceive you
- Branding is how you use your brand to influence customers
- Your logo is the visual foundation of your brand, and needs to be high resolution and appropriately reflect your brand

"Your brand is what other people say about you when you're not in the room."
~ Jeff Bezos

15

Registering your project

Another thing you need to consider is registering your project. In the introduction, I talked about how I had no clue what I was doing when I started One Planet Classrooms. I started out registering OPC as a business but soon realised this was the wrong model, then eventually worked out how to register as a Not for Profit. It is a bit of a process, and I'm not going to pretend it isn't, but depending on how far you want to take your project it could be necessary, and the good news is you will survive it!

You need to keep in mind that different countries will have different requirements, so you should investigate what to do in your country. I recommend you first think about the structure of your project and how you imagine it will operate, and then research all the options. Depending on the mission of your project and how big you intend to scale it, you would ideally investigate NFP, Charity (which is also an NFP), NGO, Social Enterprise and business structures.

This should lead you closer to what you think you would be best registered as. I suggest your first step should be taking a look at the website for your local taxation department as they are likely to have a comprehensive overview and links to further information.

Some projects might be really small and localised and won't need registering, so you might be lucky enough to avoid this whole section completely!

Some examples are:
- Enlisting a small group to clean up the local community garden
- Getting new equipment for your grade 5/6 area at school
- Getting a few people to chip in to get the floor re-varnished at the local scout hall
- Starting up a local walking group
- Setting up a FB group where people can meet and help each other

In Australia, Not for Profit is like an overarching umbrella. All charities are NFP, but not all NFP are charities. You have to register to become a charity, and you must fit into 1 of the 12 charitable purpose categories. You can only become a charity by applying and being approved by the Australian Charities and Not-For-Profits Commission (ACNC).

In 2019 in Australia, there are around 600,000 registered Not for Profits and within that around 56,000 registered charities, of which approximately 32% are registered for Deductible Gift Recipient (DGR) status, which basically means they can give tax-deductible receipts. It's actually a lot more complicated than that, and there are multiple overlapping layers, but it gives you a basic idea.

Here are the peak bodies for Australia:

ASIC - Australian Securities and Investments Commission
CAV - Consumer Affairs Victoria (each state has an equivalent)
ACNC - Australian Charities and Not-For-Profits Commission
ATO - Australian Taxation Office

If you take a look at their websites, you will get an excellent overview of how it works, but it will probably still be confusing. There are also a lot of other sites and organisations that have great information, so I suggest you become good friends with Google for this section.

If you are from outside of Australia, you will need to locate your appropriate peak bodies and make some enquiries.

Wherever you live, there will be some legal requirements so make sure you get up to speed with these.

What I have found is that all these bodies and organisations welcome questions and they really do want you to succeed, so don't be afraid to call and ask for advice or assistance.

Yes, there are rules, laws and requirements, but that's why you need to make sure you are correctly registered, and if you keep up with the requirements it's happy sailing!

As I said, this chapter provides only fundamental information, and I hope now you can see why.

Registering
- Consider the organisational structure of your project first
- Research different structures online and don't be afraid to call some peak bodies and relevant organisations
- All countries will have different peak bodies and requirements, so familiarise yourself with who and what is relevant to your area

16

Chunk it, plan it, do it!

Break it down

It is impossible to have a gigantic dream and think it will happen overnight. It won't. Even worse, if you think it will happen overnight, and it doesn't, you may feel like a failure. That's not what we want.

The key is to break it down into manageable chunks. There might be 5 steps, or there might be 100. Keep the steps achievable so that you have successes at each stage. This will keep you motivated, and you will gain strength and momentum with every success, and eventually, things will unfold exactly as they should.

It's a good idea to create a list of the main components of the project and then mark these out as headings. Then under each one, write down smaller components until you can see each one is manageable.

There are many ways to break your project down, and it doesn't matter how you do it, just that you do it in some way.

Keeping all the information in your head is a sure-fire way to get into an awful mess, and it's impossible for others to support you if they don't have access to the steps required to ensure the project is successful.

In my book 'Magnificent Kids!', I included a sample Action Plan and also a Mind Map. Both of them are based on a project to donate clothes and toys to homeless children.

Keep in mind these were designed for young people getting projects off the ground, but the principle and process will still be relevant.

At the end of the day it really doesn't matter which tools you use as long as they work for you and your project. There are dozens of different goal setting and planning templates online so do yourself a favour and have a peek.

To keep it simple, here's the action plan and mind map, along with a couple of other ideas:

Action Plan

An action plan is a template for you to write down the steps you need to take to get your project up and running. At a minimum it needs to include:

- What the action is
- The steps needed to get that action done
- Who the person is that will be responsible for doing that
- When the action needs to be completed by

As you fill it in you will see that the steps don't seem as far out of reach as you thought.

If action plans suit your style, you can easily Google more examples, and there are heaps of downloadable ones online.

There is no right or wrong way to do an action plan, but it must clearly communicate what the steps are so that anybody within your group can pick it up and follow it. Keep in mind that the date you expect to have things done by must be achievable.

Get Off The Bench!

Action Plan - Donate clothing and toys to a homeless shelter

What do we need to do?	How do we do it? (Steps)	Who is responsible?	When do we need it done by?
Make a list of local homeless shelters	Look through the local telephone directory	Susie	20/5/2019
	Do an internet search	David	20/5/2019
	Ask parents and teachers if they know of any	Susie, David, Alison & Michael	20/5/2019
	Decide which shelter to donate to	Susie, David, Alison & Michael	25/5/2019
Advertise your proposal and include a drop off point and pick up date	Create fliers	David	10/6/2019
	Hang fliers up in shops and around school	Susie	20/6/2019
	Do a letter box pamphlet drop	Michael	20/6/2019
	Announce at school assembly	Alison	24/6/2019
Collect donations	Organise parents as drivers	Susie, David, Alison & Michael	9/7/2019
Deliver donations to homeless shelter	With parents as drivers	Susie, David, Alison & Michael	31/7/2019
Advise of the outcome	Create notices of thanks and outcome	David	30/8/2019
	Hang notices up around school and shops	Susie & Michael	30/8/2019
	Announce at school assembly	Alison	30/8/2019

Mind Map

Some people find an action plan a bit too structured and prefer to think in pictures or diagrams. A mind map is a way of drawing all the main components of your project, then branching off to the smaller details.

The beauty of it is it's all there in one picture, you have a great overview, and it's a lot easier to make sense of.

You can also use a mind map to fine tune your cause. For example, if you are really passionate about helping children, you can identify some key areas and then choose one to start working on.

In this example (keep in mind this one is for kids), I have chosen homeless children to keep it consistent with the action plan, so on a mind map, it would look something like this…

Get Off The Bench!

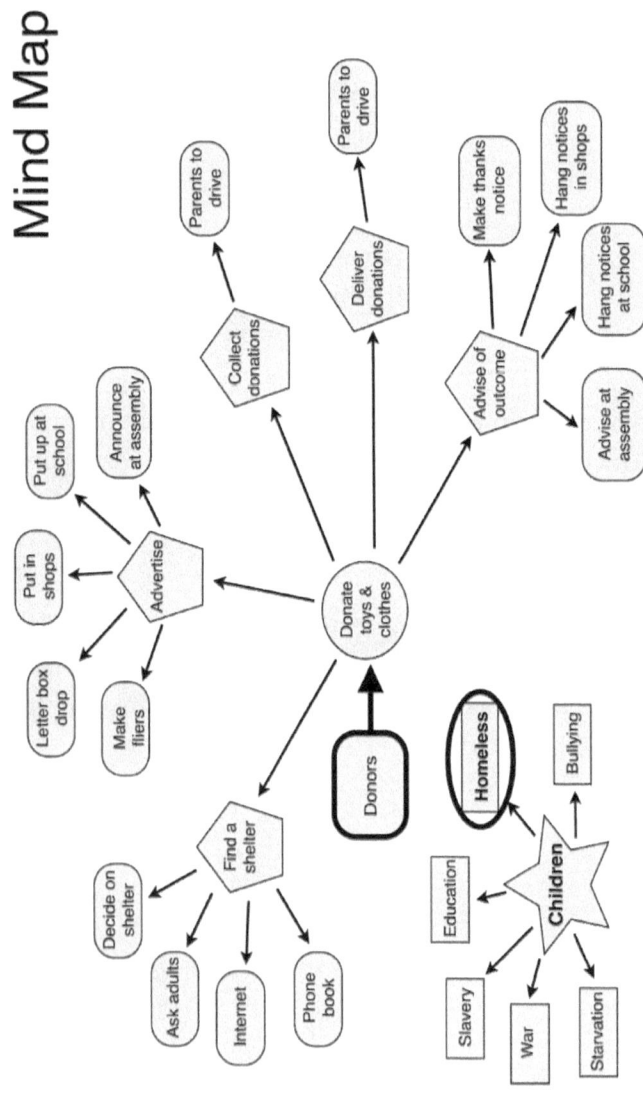

SMART

Another tool that might be helpful is SMART goals. It's commonly used in the corporate world, and it helps to keep your goals manageable. SMART is an acronym, and it unpacks like this:

S - specific, significant, stretching
M - measurable, meaningful, motivational
A - achievable, attainable, agreed upon
R - relevant, realistic
T - time-based

George T. Doran introduced this in 1981, and back then the R represented 'realistic'. Over time it has been changed and added to by multiple people, but you get the idea.

Basically, you look at your goal(s) and ask yourself if it is SMART. It keeps your goals realistic and manageable and helps you avoid setting yourself up to fail.

If you like this, then choose the words that mean the most to you. If you don't like it, then don't use it.

Personally, I never use it because for me it creates limitations to what I believe is possible. If that sounds too wishy-washy for you, then, by all means, stick to the SMART formula!

Easy as ABC...

Now, I'm about to share something that will seem quite contradictory to everything I have just said... I have included these few tools because I think if you're not sure where to start, they give you a great starting point, and you really should have some type of planning tool.

We have to keep in mind that we are all in different places within our journeys, we all believe in slightly different things, have different experiences, learn differently, and we all have specific processes that seem to work better than others.

Many years ago, I realised that for me, trying to control the steps was an absolute nightmare and by doing so I was strangling the life out of anything I was trying to achieve. I created my own formula that works a treat for me. I call it the ABC principle. It works like this:

I'm here 'ay	Let it Be	This is what I see (vision)
A	**B**	**C**

I should point out that you don't go in the order of A B C. It's best if you do **A C B**. So, if you said it out loud it would sound like this - "I'm here 'ay **A**, this is what I see **C**, let it be **B**.

I keep my eye firmly on the vision (**C**), but I like the **B** to unfold itself. To be clear, the vision has to be connected to your WHY because you need to be adaptable and flexible enough to allow the **C** to morph into what it needs to become as the project develops. But your WHY must remain intact.

When I talk about the **B** unfolding itself, it always works for me to work out the first step and do it. Then the next step instantly appears and then the next and the next and so on. It's like somebody laying one paver at a time ahead of your feet, and when you step on that one, the next one appears.

Having said that, within the **B** you need to be (B) enthusiastic, open, energetic, aware, opportunistic, adaptable, respectful, engaged and a multitude of other proactive and positive things. You have to be immersed and active without being inflexibly controlling.

This is the way I work best, but this might not be for you at all, and that's OK. It's really important we know what works best for us and to be honest, most people I know use the traditional action plans, mind maps and SMART goals.

But this is your project, so you find the best fit for you.

Big picture…

Now let's get back to the big picture and get a few headings underway. These headings will be essential components of your project, but are likely to need a number of smaller actions below each one.

Here are a few examples:
- Build a website
- Build a vision and a story
- Gather supporters
- Apply for funding
- Get permits
- Register NFP
- Recruit volunteers
- Buy a bus
- Secure office space

Q. What are 5 big picture actions you need to take?

Q. What is the first step?
(Commit to do this in the next 24-48hrs)

IN A NUTSHELL...

Actions
- The first step is always the hardest
- Do It Anyway!
- Create headings then break them down into smaller components/actions

- Decide which action tool works best for you...
Action Plan
Mind Map
SMART goals
ABC Principle

Or try them all and/or any other tool(s) you can find

"Take Action!
An inch of movement will bring you
closer to your goals than
a mile of intention."
~ Michael Hyatt

17

Maintaining momentum

You have to continue to be innovative, flexible and adaptable. If you don't, you stagnate and disappear.

Selling your idea is like an ongoing campaign rather than a one-off sale, and you have to keep beating the drum. You can't just have one information session and think everybody will just jump in. It doesn't work like that. Keep the fire burning and the momentum building.

If possible, create a list of micro jobs people can do so they don't feel trapped by major commitments. This also gives them tastes of success, and they are likely to come back for more. Successes feel great!

Consistency is HUGE. Be very consistent with everything and follow up on promises in a timely manner. People lose confidence very quickly if others wax and wane in their communications and enthusiasm.

You showing up regularly tells people you (and your idea) are safe, reliable, and here to stay.

You need to be seen. You can't hide behind your computer and use only the power of written word to be persuasive. People need connection: they need to feel important and feel seen. Show up at places so people can have a personal meet and greet. And be nice! People may forget what you said, but they will never forget how you made them feel.

Daily action - you need to live and breathe your idea like it is an extension of you. It has to be aligned with your values: it has to become integrated into your life and become an unconscious habit. Big ideas don't just happen; they need time to be nurtured and fine-tuned. A great habit of getting into is to do at least one thing for your project every single day.

What makes an even better habit, is making your project the first thing you do each day, before you even think about your paid job (if you still have one), your emails or any other de-energising stuff. It only has to be 15 minutes if that's all you can spare. By the time we get home at night, despite our good intentions, we are way too tired to invest in our project with a clear mind, and we have no room left for creativity. Creativity is a vital part of getting your project off the ground and maintaining its longevity, and it's a huge contributor to your vision.

Remain as transparent as possible. I'm not suggesting your financials should be spread across everybody's kitchen table, but you can publicly share some of your difficulties, your aims, small successes, engaging stories, vulnerabilities, disappointments and anything else that supporters may have also felt themselves. This helps them to feel like they are on the journey with you. They feel like part of a movement that is growing and expanding, and when people ride the waves with you, they are more deeply and emotionally connected.

Demonstrated achievement is king! Everybody wants to see proven outcomes. I have consistently used demonstrated achievement as my greatest marketing tool. You can have all the big words and hype, and the flashiest paraphernalia possible, but if people can't see regular and consistent achievements and outcomes they will soon feel like a number contributing to a stagnant cause.

You must keep having achievements, or at least demonstrated progress, or supporters will drop off. A great way to achieve this is to break down bigger events or projects to bite size ones, where each can showcase success. Even the tiniest amount of progress keeps people engaged because of the sense of movement.

IN A NUTSHELL...

Maintaining momentum
- You have to keep being innovative, flexible and adaptable
- Selling your idea is like a campaign, rather than a one-off sale – keep beating the drum
- Create micro jobs so supporters have lots of small successes
- Consistency is HUGE – this tells people you (and your idea) are safe, reliable, and here to stay
- You need to be seen. Get out and meet and greet. And be nice!
- Daily action – live and breathe your idea like it is an extension of you
- Be transparent – this helps people feel like they are on the journey with you
- Demonstrated achievement is king! Everybody wants to see outcomes.

18

And finally...

Well, there you have it. I wish I had this book 20 years ago - I would have actually started rather than only dreamed about things!

Hopefully, it has been helpful to you and helped to fine tune your project. Setting up a project may seem a little overwhelming, but it doesn't have to be. It really depends on the size of the project and how complex it is. But where there's a will, there's a way.

If you want to start an NFP organisation that will have global reaches and potentially have a huge impact, then yes you will have to work a little harder. But the reward will be just as big!

On the other hand, if you want to make a difference without all the fuss, there are many things you can do, on a much smaller scale, that can have a significant impact on the lives you directly and indirectly touch, as I have already pointed out in the introduction.

When we pick up a pebble and throw it into a pond, we no longer have the pebble. It has left our hand, and we are now unable to control its ripple. But imagine if one of your 'pebbles' was talking to a group of friends about the plight of starving kids in Africa.

Perhaps your friends appear indifferent to your concerns, but without you knowing, one friend goes home and talks about what you said with her family over dinner. The friend's son, sitting at the dinner table becomes so touched by the conversation that he starts to ask WHY?

He is so driven by his WHY that his life and academic choices soon lead him to become an International Aid worker. He spends the next 15 years travelling to and from Africa and in this time manages to set up sustainable produce gardens in hundreds of villages.

Now, how important is every little pebble we drop into a pond?

Very!

There are 3 things you need to do:

1 - Dream it

2 - Decide to do it

3 - Take action

The first step is always the hardest!

One day
or
Day one

You decide...

~ unknown

About the Author...

KERRYN VAUGHAN

Kerryn is a speaker, international author, singer/songwriter, trainer, mentor and podcast host. Her book 'Magnificent Kids!' was the catalyst to her founding the global organisation One Planet Classrooms, which facilitates projects to relieve poverty-induced suffering, predominantly in Africa. Such projects include clean water solutions, solar power, sustainable projects, feminine hygiene & empowerment initiatives, as well as the sponsorship of more than 180 school children.

One Planet Classrooms was initially set up to facilitate Skype sessions between classrooms in Africa and Australia, but this was an epic fail! At that point, she could have given up and walked away from the whole idea, but the lessons from that have been the driving force to reframe failure, keep going and trust that the world needs what you have to offer.

For many years Kerryn has been coaching people to get their ideas and projects off the ground, and currently, this forms a solid part of Girls With Hammers, a business she co-founded in 2018, which focuses on women's empowerment through conferences, workshops and mentoring. With loads of success stories under her belt, she knows only too well how to help people find their voice and unlock their magnificence, and delivers this in a brutally honest kick-ass way that only Kerryn can.

Kerryn is a highly skilled inspirational speaker who has presented at numerous events & conferences, both in Australia and internationally, typically speaking about empowerment, creating a better world and standing in your truth. Not surprising, Kerryn's life mantra states, **'If we can make a difference, why wouldn't we?'**

Notes...

www.ingramcontent.com/pod-product-compliance
Lightning Source LLC
Chambersburg PA
CBHW020426010526
44118CB00010B/436